The Progress of Economic Doctrine in England in the Eighteenth Century

WILLIAM CUNNINGHAM

1891

TABLE OF CONTENTS

THE PROGRESS OF ECONOMIC DOCTRINE IN ENGLAND IN THE EIGHTEENTH CENTURY

By universal consent Adam Smith stands out as the founder of modern political economy. He so entirely recast it that the ordinary student of economic doctrine is satisfied to trace the progress from his time, just as the astronomer marks a new departure in the system of Copernicus, and modern philosophy took a new shape at the hands of Kant. In each of those cases, however, it is possible to note anticipations and suggestions in the thoughts of previous writers; and those, whose curiosity tempts them to go behind The Wealth of Nations on some tentative exploration, are not unlikely to be surprised to find that so many men of wide knowledge and accurate habits of thought had already devoted themselves to the study of economic phenomena. It is a literary problem of no little interest to discover how far these various writers led up to The Wealth of Nations, and to discriminate precisely wherein the secret of Adam Smith's marked superiority really lay. The impression he made upon his contemporaries, and the unique position which his book maintains at the present day, prove beyond dispute that he was incomparably superior to all his predecessors; but it is not easy to account for the difference. We cannot detect the characteristic feature in his work by comparing him, not always to his advantage, with some previous writer who wrote brilliantly upon a special point; and we can only hope to discover it by reviewing the progress of economic doctrine for many years before he wrote, and thus attempting to mark the precise nature of the new contribution which enabled him to transform the study so completely.

It is of course clear, that circumstances favoured a great advance in economic doctrine during the eighteenth century, since there was so much progress in industrial, commercial, and agricultural afairs. The phenomena connected with the increase of wealth were more obvious, and a keen observer like Adam Smith who had frequent intercourse with practical men, was in an excellent position for reflecting on the causes of this progress; but after all, these changes, though decided, had been slow; other observers had noted and described the more important facts, and traced out the causes that were at work. A general condition of this kind, though it accounts for the progress of the study as a whole, does not help to explain the special eminence of Adam Smith. We shall find a better guide if we take the revolutionary period as a starting-point and look at the mere form and divisions of the subject in the treatises which were published then, and compare them with The Wealth of Nations.

1. Davenant and Petty were writers of extraordinary acuteness. Their works are full of careful statistics, and of accurate and ingenious remark. Numberless phrases can be culled from their works which anticipate the reasonings of later writers, but the very titles of their chief books show that their view of the subject is restricted. They deal with the expenses of government as the one important topic; Petty's great work is A Treatise of Taxes and Contributions, which was written with special reference to the fiscal administration of Ireland; Davenant compiled An Essay on Ways and Means of Supplying the War. The central thoughts with both are the expenses of government and the modes of defraying them; though from this starting-point they proceed to treat the subject with much judgment and skill, the form which all the problems take is affected by the point of view from which they look at them.

Since these economists dealt primarily with English revenue, there were three main funds to be considered; the increase of treasure which was necessary in order to defray the expenses of war and thus to render the Government secure against emergencies; the increase of commerce and of the customs; and the increase of the wealth of the landed class who contributed such a large proportion of the revenue of the country. Bullion gave the means of gathering and amassing treasure; and if trade were so managed as to afford an opportunity for accumulating treasure there seemed to be plain evidence that the Government was in good case; and the Balance of Trade apparently offered a simple means of estimating how far this was so. The customs had been an important source of revenue from the time of Edward III.; and the resources of the landowners as a fund for possible taxation had been kept in view since William noted the assessment of every estate in Domesday book.

The economists of the Revolution era also looked below the funds from which contributions were paid, and tried to analyze the causes which might keep the funds amply supplied; they were ready to look at the factors which go to the production of national prosperity—factors which facilitated the cultivation of land, and which worked up the manufactured goods which we exported to other lands. Locke laid stress upon the productive cause of value; while Gregory King and others insisted that labour depended for its effect on the fund which employed it, and studied the condition of various ranks of society with special reference to their ability to save capital. Capital, too, was able to utilize and send to market the results obtained through the productive power of nature; and thus attention was not exclusively given to the funds from which taxes were defrayed, but also to the factors by which these funds were brought into being and maintained.

When economists thus examined the factors which produced national prosperity it became possible for them to compare the working of these factors in various countries even though these countries presented many differences. The English method of taxation from the land was repugnant to French subjects, who had, however, no strong objection to an excise which the English freeholders hated as the worst of tyrannies. Differences of national temperament rendered it difficult to compare the fiscal policy of the two Governments or to discuss the relative advantages of either method; but after all the source, from which revenue was ultimately derived in both cases, was the material wealth of the subjects. In both cases labour, capital, and land were the factors which went to produce it, though they might contribute in different proportions to the prosperity of different lands; and hence the respective advantages and disadvantages of two or more countries could be discussed and compared.

2. During the first sixty years of the eighteenth century the financial condition and the fiscal possibilities of England were still the chief topics to which economic writers addressed themselves, and not without reason. Although there had been as we see now, a remarkable growth in many directions there were not a few causes for grave anxiety about the time of the Seven Years' War. The growth of the National Debt and the impossibility of finding new sources of taxation alarmed more than one statesman, and there were not a few economists who took a pessimistic view of the condition of the country. Their writings, however, are of far more interest from the light they throw on passing events, and from the statistics they contain, than from any very remarkable advance in economic doctrine. They all start from the old standpoint. In all cases their writing was of practical interest and their practical interest was that of rendering the nation prosperous and powerful as compared with other nations.

Malachy Postlethwayt was the most celebrated of these writers. Quite in the old manner he compares the commercial and colonial policy of England with that of Holland and of France, and tries to show how the British system might be improved, so as to outdo their rivals. Others were alarmed, not at the prosperity of our ancient rival, but at the pressure of indirect taxation. There were pamphlets without end as to the absolute necessity of living on the national income; and the failure of the Sinking Fund filled economists with the wildest forebodings as to the future of the country and the continued pressure of debt. There were others who were more concerned at the indirect effects of this indebtedness. Large debts meant heavy interest, and heavy interest meant that commerce was hampered by large custom duties. This was the cry of Sir Matthew Decker, Richardson, and Fauquier; and in their enthusiasm for an unfettered commerce they were apparently inclined to sweep away all the expedients for directing trade. Indeed one main objection which was urged to their schemes was that they practically involved having free ports, and that this might lead to the cessation of any governmental efforts to guide the direction of capital. But though Richardson and Decker are apparently in favour of free trade, the manner in which they talk about the Balance of Trade, goes to show that they were still on the platform of those who were considering the national prosperity as their main object, and chiefly interested in national wealth because it was the primary source of national power.

In order to judge of the condition of any of the funds from which the revenue was drawn, and thus of the expediency of the rules then current for its conduct, it was convenient either to measure these resources as completely as possible, or to take some group of phenomena as typical of the rest. Torrents of schemes were issued from the press, containing wild guesses as to possible amounts, and wilder interpretations of these uncertain data. The Mercator and the British Merchant are full of figures, and Massie's numerous tracts are crammed with calculations; but the methods of statistical study were little appreciated, and few of these writers seem to have made serious efforts to check the accuracy of the figures on which they relied. Petty, of course, stands by himself as a pioneer; his work was of unexampled excellence, but those who imitated his studies were very far from following his example. In some cases those who did not attempt to compute the changes in England as a whole were satisfied to take one branch of trade as exemplifying all the rest. There was still one department of economic life which had a peculiar interest for Englishmen, and which was treated as of special importance—this was the maintenance of shipping as the means of offence and defence; but this was regarded as an object of policy towards which the Government were bound to direct the three factors which increased wealth. It was a matter of public importance; and the art of government, as it was conceived in the eighteenth century, consisted in so guiding the private interest of individuals that they might work for the public good. In the sixteenth century moralists had written of private interest as if it were invariably hostile to public advantage. Men were expected to carry on their trade in a public-spirited fashion and not to regard their private lucre; but in the eighteenth century the force of self-interest was recognized as a power that was rather indifferent than hostile to the public good, so that it seemed as if a very moderate amount of direction might be brought to bear, and thus induce men who were guided by self-interest alone to carry on their business in a manner that accorded with public prosperity.

Although it was particularly important to measure the improvement or decay of any of the factors which made for the production of wealth, it was by no means easy to do so. Political arithmeticians could, however. note symptoms which were specially striking; and they could look either at the results of our industry (agricultural and manufacturing) or at the conditions under which it was carried on,—these conditions having reference both to the facilities for procuring capital and to the effectiveness of Labour. These three points were most easily examined by considering three criteria, first the Balance of Trade, as showing the profitableness of our commercial intercourse with various countries; second, the rate of interest as showing the facility with which capital might be procured, either for agriculture, manufacture, or commerce; thirdly, the condition of the poor, as showing how far the labourers could maintain themselves and add by their work to the wealth of the country, or how far they were dependent on funds procured by others.

3. These were the main topics of discussion among the economists in the middle of the eighteenth century in so far as they dealt with anything larger than the technique of particular arts or of commercial transactions as a whole. There was plenty of writing on these special points, as there had been in the preceding century; but little of it is of first-rate importance with regard to the general progress of economic study. This was gradually penetrating more deeply, however; and the writers of the middle of the eighteenth century were able to neglect subjects which their predecessors at the time of the Revolution had put into the forefront. Since the expenses of government could be defrayed by borrowing, the policy of hoarding treasure was no longer of importance; it simply drops out of sight altogether. Though attention was still constantly directed to the Balance of Trade, the significance which was attached to it had entirely altered. In the seventeenth century, it was supposed to measure the possible accumulations of treasure; in the eighteenth it was treated as a criterion of the flourishing condition of our industry. If we parted with more goods than we received, it was clear that we were supplying ourselves successfully and had something over to sell; if we were buying more goods than we sent abroad, it seemed to show that we were unable to provide for our own subsistence. The accuracy of the information supplied by this index may certainly be questioned. In the present day the movements of capital and

interest to and from foreign lands render it absolutely valueless; but it is clear that those who used it as an index were on a diferent plane of thought from the writers who had laid stress on the form in which the balance was defrayed and the accumulation of bullion to which a 'gaining' trade would lead.

There are other matters in regard to which we may detect a change of view, for we hear far less about the high rental of land as a matter of congratulation. This was perhaps partly due to a change of fiscal policy; the land-tax had been assessed permanently, and there was less possibility of expansion in the revenue derived from this source. But it was also due to the fact that though the theory of rent was not generally understood, there was a clearer apprehension of the truth that the production from the soil was primarily dependent on the capital employed in improvements, and that if capital were plentiful, agriculture and all connected with it would be flourishing too. The time of rural improvement had begun, and capitalists under the inducement offered by the bounty on export were sinking their capital in land. There was no need for special anxiety about this source of taxation. Besides this, Walpole had reorganized another of these funds—the Customs; for he had effected a revolution in our tariff; he entirely reconstructed it with a view of promoting our industrial prosperity, and did not regard it merely as a source of revenue, but chiefly as an instrument for directing industry, or stimulating it. It thus came about that the three topics which had engrossed attention in the seventeenth century, the balance of trade, high rents, and the customs, entirely lost their old importance. Though the old subjects are discussed and many of the old phrases are retained, there is a marked advance in the thoroughness of economic studies in the middle of the eighteenth century, as compared even with those of the revolutionary period and certainly with the writers of still earlier times.

4. Indeed, while there was the same desire as of old to guide the industry and commerce of the country so as to promote its power, there are general indications that men were beginning to feel a difficulty in applying any of their tests rigidly, and deciding what would prove beneficial. Some were inclined to collect additional infomation, to fall back upon the history of some department of industry for a considerable number of years, to note its periods of prosperity or of failure and to try and assign the causes which had affected it in either case. The most remarkable and complete of such treatises is John Smith's Chronicon-Rusticum-Commerciale, or Memoirs of Wool, a book which gives an exceedingly detailed account, based on documentary evidence, of the growth of this staple trade. The policy which was pursued in one period is contrasted with the line that was taken at another time, and contemporary literature is drawn on in the fullest possible manner, with the view of indicating the bearings of the change.

These careful historical monographs had a very direct bearing on some of the practical questions of the time. It may be said that all the inconvenience then felt about the coinage was ultimately connected with the difficulty of fixing on the best standard of value. A flood of light was thrown on this subject by the excellent work of Bishop Fleetwood. He had preached a sermon, which had been one of the first utterances that called attention to the deficiencies of our coinage, and the evils of a clipped currency; and the manner in which he discussed the variations of silver as a standard of value showed that he had clearer views on the subject than many of his contemporaries. It was comparatively easy to prove that coins could not be rated very differently from the exchange value of the bullion they contained, but it was not so easy to see what determined the value of the precious metals as bullion. The difficulty was rendered greater since men argued that while other commodities were naturally sought after because they supported human life, or ministered to individual human needs, silver was only prized because mankind had agreed to use it as money. Locke was a mercantilist to the backbone, but so far from regarding money as the only kind of wealth he is inclined to deny that it was of the nature of wealth at all, except by mere agreement. Under such circumstances it was plausible to maintain that the same convention which caused it to be wealth, definitely assigned its value in exchange. No serious attempt could be made at adopting a single standard for the coinage and keeping to it till the fact that the value of silver bullion varied with regard to the other precious metals, and with regard to commodities of every sort was fully recognized. Fleetwood's Chronicon Preciosum takes the form of a discussion on a point of casuistry. 'The statutes of s certain college,' he says, '(to the observation of which, every one is sworn, when admitted fellow) vacating a fellowship if the fellow has an estate in land of inheritance or a perpetual pension of £5 per annum, I desire you would be pleased to give me your answer to the following questions, when I have first told you that the college was founded between the years 1440 and 1460.' The third question was the important one; it ran as follows:—'Whether he who is actually possessed of an estate of £6 per annum as money and things go now, may safely take that oath, upon presumption that £6 now, is not worth what £5 was, when that statute was made.' He goes on to show that gold and silver had both fallen in value with regard to commodities, but that they had kept about, though not quite, the same proportion towards one another. The discussion of the silver coinage is very careful, and there is a mass of facts in the two chapters in which he proves that silver had fallen very greatly in value as compared both with corn and with the rates and wages.

Both of these works give evidence of exhaustive research and of intelligent criticism. In neither respect are they really rivalled by the extraordinary collection of information on all matters connected with English industry and commerce, which was originally published in 1764 by Mr. Anderson. The Annals of Commerce are a monument of painstaking industry, and there is no branch of the subject in regard to which they do not render invaluable service, but the work is primarily a work of reference; it is a collection of materials which seems to be almost inexhaustible, and later students cannot be suihciently grateful for the painstaking industry of this careful historian; but since the work is arranged in the unpretentious form of annals, it does not pretend to be more than a storehouse of materials, and though there is some acute criticism, the book is less effective as a whole than might have been the case il there had been a serious attempt to string these disjointed fragments into a connected history.

The one man who united a profound knowledge of economic literature, as it had grown up in the two preceding centuries, with a keen interest in the practical economic difficulties of his time, was Joseph Massie. He had spared no expense in forming a collection which contained some fifteen hundred tracts and treatises; and the study of these had served to make him a discriminating critic. In particular he had felt that numbers of pamphleteers, who pretended to be arguing for the good of the public, were really actuated by some selfish and personal motive. Statements of fact in many cases required careful examination; and in not a few instances the writing was so specious, and the motive of private interest was so plain that it was necessary to discount much of the argument. To his mind the real need seemed to be a criterion which would enable us to distinguish the national from the personal interest. His scheme for attaining this desirable end was thorough and painstaking, as he believed it might be reached not by trusting to a single criterion, but by an exhaustive examination of the phenomena of industrial and commercial life so as to establish 'commercial knowledge upon fixed principles.' 'There is no other way,' he says, 'to acquire a satisfactory knowledge of the state, andc., of the manufactures and trade of this kingdom than by treating of each branch separately, so that their increase, decrease, influence, andc., may appear; for every part must be distinctly known or the whole cannot be well understood.' Even with the pains and attention which he had given to the matter, he had found it impossible to carry on his researches in the thorough fashion which he deemed desirable, though he was by no means inclined to pursue a subject with pedantic curiosity beyond the limits that were needed for bringing out points of lasting importance. 'So that facts, circumstances, and controversies, which either never were nationally interesting in themselves, or have been rendered useless in that respect by length of time, should not be inserted in a general work that is intended to promote commercial knowledge; for there ought to be a keeping of proportion in books as well as in pictures; and the several parts of a subject should be so treated of, that the mind may discover which are the principal objects therein, as the eye is enabled to distinguish the principal figures in an historical picture.' But though he was so discriminating, his scheme of studying each branch was extraordinarily thorough; he proposed to divide his historical account of every branch of manufacture into sixteen heads, under one or other of which, fragments of information might be classified, in the hope that the whole account would sooner or later be made sufficiently complete.

The mere fact that Massie regarded such an investigation as necessary in order to discriminate what was really of national concern, shows that he was by no means satisfied with the rough and ready schemes of national success or decay which were based on some particular set of figures. His whole appeal for investigation is an implied confession that his contemporaries had no satisfactory means of determining where the national interest really lay. His very attitude is a condemnation of the methods of reasoning which satisfied the ordinary writer, or were bandied in the House of Commons. But despite this, he is still on the standpoint of the Mercantile System. He believed that it was possible to attain to a knowledge of principles which should tend to increase the prosperity and power of the country, and that when these principles were detected it was necessary to carry them out, and to take active measures to check the private interest which conflicted with them. His attitude comes out curiously in his criticism of Sir Matthew Decker's scheme of taxation. He shows that the abolition of customs, which might favour trade in some ways, could not be accomplished without repealing all tariffs and thus discarding the instrument by which trade could be directed into channels of national advantage. When he had pointed out that this was implied in the proposal he felt that he had demolished the whole thing, for he had the firmest conviction of the necessity for suppressing private interest and regulating trade for the national weal.

5. Other thinkers tried to frame a satisfactory system for promoting the power of the country by thinking out a scheme in which the different factors might work harmoniously; they relied not so much on new investigation as on more careful reflection. It was obvious that the regulations which had been made for encouraging manufactures and increasing the customs might be detrimental to the rent of land. Such for example was the case with the laws which prohibited the export of wool or encouraged the importation of pig-iron from America. Both the welfare of the landed interest and of the manufacturers were important objects of policy, but one conflicted with the other. What favoured the one might be detrimental to the other; hence it might frequently be necessary to balance the landed against the manufacturing interest, and try to give each its due development. Arthur Young was constantly complaining, under the

influence of the French Physiocrats, that manufactures were unduly developed and the agricultural interest too much neglected. The right course, as he conceived, would be to develop agriculture first of all to its fullest extent, with an easy confidence that manufactures and commerce would follow naturally in its wake. But whenever we get this idea of a due proportion between the various parts of the social fabric, we must have some ideal or form to which we desire to make our practice conform. The eighteenth century had a keen eye to proportion in the structure of buildings, and eagerly followed the classical type while adapting it to modern requirements; and in the same way their discussions of the due proportion between manufactures and agriculture imply some more or less definite conception of an ideal economic condition which should possess in its highest form the element of stability.

Sir James Steuart, who wrote in 1764, was an author who deliberately devoted himself to working out such an ideal. He set himself to discover 'a good plan of economy' by a wide course of observation and reflection. 'The speculative person,' he says, 'who removed from the practice extracts the principle of this science from observation and reflection, should divest himself as far as possible of every prejudice in favour of established opinions however reasonable when examined relatively to particular nations; he must do his utmost to become a citizen of the world, comparing customs, examining minutely institutions which appear alike when in different countries they are found to produce different effects; he should examine the cause of such differences with the utmost diligence and attention; it is from such inquiries that the true principles are discovered. Not only must he take account of the present but of the past, and by so doing he may be able to follow "the regular progress of mankind from great simplicity to complicated refinement." ' In this way he believed that he might obtain a science of which the principles were 'universally true,' and it would then be the business of the statesman to direct the industry and commerce of any given people in the closest practicable accord with those principles. 'The principal object of this science is to secure a certain fund of subsistence for all the inhabitants, to obviate every circumstance which may render it precarious, to provide everything necessary for supplying the wants of the society, and to employ the inhabitants in such a manner as naturally to create reciprocal relations and dependencies between them, so as to make their several interests lead them to supply one another with their reciprocal wants.' It must, however, be confessed that in plunging into this sea of 'metapolitical' speculation, Sir James Steuart fails to attain very important results. He did, indeed, make important contributions to particular doctrines; but his general art of political economy and his general maxims are for the most part mere truisms, for which he is himself inclined to apologize; and his imaginary history of the development of human civilization is but dull reading after all. He had come deeply under the influence of Montesquieu, and the effect of the Spirit of Laws is obvious over and over again,—in particular, in the attention he gives to the spirit of a people. 'The great art of governing,' he says, 'is to divest oneself of prejudices and attachments to particular opinions, particular classes, and above all to particular persons, to consult the spirit of the people, to give way to it in appearance, and in so doing to give it a turn capable of inspiring those sentiments which may induce them to relish the change which an alteration of circumstances has rendered necessary.' Statesmen were to guide the people by reason and not by artifice, for experience showed that a people 'tricked into an imposition, though expedient for their prosperity, will oppose violently at another time a like measure even when essential to their preservation.'

In thus guiding the citizens towards the economic ideal, the statesman was called upon to deal with purely self-regarding interests. The principle of competition is abundantly recognized throughout his treatise as usually operative in all commercial transactions. 'The best way to govern a society, and to engage everyone to conduct himself according to a plan, is for the statesman to form a system of administration, the most consistent possible with the interest of every individual, and never to flatter himself that his people will be brought to act in general, and in matters which purely regard the public from any other principle than private interest. This is the utmost length to which I pretend to carry my position. As to what regards the merit and demerit of actions in general, I think it fully as absurd to say, that no action is truly virtuous, as to affirm that none is really vicious.

'It might perhaps be expected that, in treating of politics, I should have brought in public spirit also, as a principle of action; whereas all I require with respect to this principle is merely a restraint from it, and even this is perhaps too much to be taken for granted. Were public spirit, instead of private utility, to become the spring of action in the individuals of a well-governed state, I apprehend it would spoil all. Let me explain myself.

'Public spirit, in my way oi treating this subject, is as superfluous in the governed, as it ought to be all-powerful in the statesman: at least, if it is not altogether superfluous, it is fully as much so, as miracles are in a religion once fully established. Both are admirable at setting out, but would shake everything loose, were they continue to be common and familiar. Were miracles wrought every day the laws of nature would no longer be laws: and were everyone to act for the public and neglect himself the statesman would be bewildered, and the supposition is ridiculous.

'I expect, therefore, that every man is to act for his own interest in what regards the public, and, politically speaking, every one ought to do so. It is the combination of every private interest which forms the public good, and of this the public, that is the statesmen only, can judge.'

The opposition between private interest and public good is really reduced to a minimum in such a doctrine as this, but Sir James is still definitely within the circle of the Mercantilist's ideas, since he holds so strongly that it is wise for the statesman to direct industry and commerce into the right channels; though he realizes, as few of his predecessors had done, that this is a most difficult and delicate operation.

6. The way was now fully prepared for the gemius of Adam Smith to give a new turn to the old inquiries, and thus to revolutionize the whole nature of economic doctrine. Like all strokes of genius, what he did was extremely simple, and it was none the less a stroke of genius because the work of preceding writers had so far paved the way that they public were able to appreciate the merits of The Wealth of Nations at the moment when it appeared. He was prepared to go one step further than Sir James Steuart. The latter had aimed at, though he did not attain, an ideal scheme of national economy, while Adam Smith held that no such system was necessary. His predecessors had believed that the statesman must play upon private interests so as to force them to conduce to the public good, and the maintenance of national power. In Sir James Steuart this guiding aim becomes a mere abstraction, and the chief point to be considered in adjusting that aim is another abstraction—the spirit of the people. Truly the mercantile system was ready to vanish away. Adam Smith did not attempt to correct any previous system of economy, he was content to insist that all systems were idle, if not positively noxious. Other writers had begun with the requirements of the State, and had worked back to the funds in the possession of the people, from which these requirements could be supplied. Adam Smith approached the subject from the other end. The first object of political economy, as he understood it, was, 'to provide a plentiful revenue or subsistence for the people,' the second was, 'to supply the State or commonwealth, with a revenue sufficient for the public services.' He simply discussed the subject of wealth; its bearing on the condition of the State appeared an afterthought. His great achievement lay in isolating the conception of national wealth, while previous writers had treated it in conscious subordination to the idea of national power.

So far as 'political economy considered as a branch of a science of a statesman' was concerned, it was now possible to regard material wealth as a main object in view; and if this was the main object in view, then the systems of policy which had preferred one kind of wealth to another, or one kind of trade to another, on political grounds, had simply lost their raison d'être. The system of natural liberty was the necessary outcome of the new turn which Adam Smith had given to the old problem. We have already seen, in connexion with Massie and Sir James Steuart, how little his ablest predecessors were satisfied with the expedients then in vogue; and when Adam Smith propounded the new doctrine that all efforts to direct trade wisely were labour thrown away, the public of his age were ready to give him a hearing and to accept the new principles which followed from concentrating attention not on power, but on the necessaries and conveniences of life.

At no previous time perhaps, would it have been possible to proclaim this doctrine with any chance of success, but the circumstances of the day supplied the conditions which his principle assumes. The local obstacles to the fluidity of capital were for the most part disappearing. Even in towns like Hull, where the trading corporations had had an uninterrupted tenure of power for centuries, their influence was coming to an end, and the incorporated companies for commerce and for industry were no longer so exclusive or no longer so important. Everywhere there was freedom for internal commerce, and thus capital was able to flow into any direction which the rate of profit rendered attractive to the capitalist, and where as that very rate of profit showed, there was opportunity for developing some neglected side of national wealth. Till this was approximately the case, it would not have been so easy to urge that the system of natural liberty was most consonant with national prosperity.

In regard to other individual factors, there was no such free play; the system of natural liberty was realized in a somewhat one-sided fashion. The English law of entail and the custom of common-field cultivation, sufficed in many places to prevent the improvement ofthe land. The laws of settlement placed crushing restrictions on the fluidity of labour, and the laws against combinations put the workers at a terrible disadvantage in competing for better wages. Adam Smith was prompt to denounce these evils, but the British public were not prompt to recognize them. It was not till the progress of the industrial revolution had demonstrated the frightful mischief of a partial adoption of natural liberty—that is to say, the adoption of this principle in regard to one factor of production, while it is wholly disregarded in relation to another—that the conditions of society were rendered more completely accordant to those which Adam Smith's principle assumes.

7. By isolating wealth, and the causes of wealth, as a subject of study which could be pursued apart from the investigation of other political phenomena, Adam Smith laid the foundation of modern political economy. It was in this way that he differed from all his predecessors, so far as I have been able to examine them. There are two different sides from which we may obtain confirmatory evidence in regard to this characteristic feature of his work. We may note (i) the manner in which he treats previous writers, and (ii) the reception of his book hy his contemporaries.

Firstly, the whole force of his criticism both of the Mercantilists and of the

Physiocrats depends on the assumption that they were discussing economic problems in the more definite sense in which he himself regarded them. But this assumption, which is never explicitly stated, was wholly untrue. The English Mercantilists were considering how the power of this country might be promoted relatively to that of other nations. The object of their system was not absolute progress anywhere but relative superiority to our political neighbours. Their commercial jealousy followed from political distrust; and Adam Smith appears to admit that from this point of view, their reasoning was right. 'The wealth,' he says, 'of neighbouring nations, however, though dangerous in war and politics is certainly advantageous in trade. In a state of hostility it may enable our enemies to maintain fleets and armies superior to our own, but in a state of peace and commerce, it must likewise enable them to exchange with us, to our mutual advantage. As the Mercantilists were avowedly writing from a political standpoint they were bound to consider how to guard against these dangers. Adam Smith in criticising them persistently refuses to take their point of view. He assumes that they were trying to devise means for increasing wealth, or as they would have said, riches, as an end in itself, while every page of their writing showed that they were doing nothing of the kind. As a consequence, his vigorous attack misrepresents them strangely. They had attached political importance to treasure, but it would be easy to show that they rather underrated than overrated the importance of gold for commercial purposes and as an element of riches. And so with all the other points of their policy; they did not imagine they increased the riches or wealth of the country by the restrictions on colonial trade, but they did think that they increased its power, and the events of the eighteenth century went a long way to prove they were right.

Similarly with the Physiocrsts; when Quesnay spoke of agriculture as productive, and of all manufacturers and commercial men as sterile, he is not considering the means of procuring the necessaries and conveniences of life; he is pointing to a source from which in the progress of the society, an agricultural state may derive a permanent revenue with the least possible inconvenience to the citizens in their ordinary avocations. He points to an unearned 'increment from land,' though economic science had not so far advanced as to enable him to name it quite definitely. Adam Smith assumes in his criticism that Quesnay is really discussing the causes of the increase of national wealth—the necessaries and conveniences of life—as they act in any country, and that he represents the produce of the land as the sole source; but Quesnay's maxima were avowedly devised for an agricultural realm, and he explicitly notes that the scheme would be inapplicable to small maritime states which are dependent on commerce. He was not discussing the growth of riches, but the most convenient source of taxation in a special community. But Adam Smith's criticism was not less damaging because it was quite irrelevant.

The misrepresentations of both these systems are glaring, and of course it can never be possible to decide with certainty how far Adam Smith mistook the purport of these writers and how far he was unfair. But when we take account of the acumen and character of the man, it is as difficult to the historian as it was to contemporaries in Paris to believe that his misrepresentations were unconscious. The story of Adam Smith's relations with Hume, shows that he was neither distinguished for frankness nor moral courage; and there is little reason to plead for him as a judicial critic, if an adequate motive can be assigned for the misrepresentation of his predecessors; and the motive is not far to seek. His treatise was thoroughly practical; he may well have believed as others had done, that the whole scheme of Government interference, and the whole fiscal policy which rested on it, was bad. Under the circumstances he rightly desired to sweep it away and to have the revenue system altered in accordance with the maxims which he had adopted from M. Moreau de Beaumont. But by attacking the mercantile principles on which our existing system was founded, and by discrediting the Physiocratic principles which had been stated by Locke. and had become popular in France, he could hope to clear the way for the reforms which he approved, and which were, in some of the most obvious points, effected by Pitt. He seems to have had a practical object in view; the alterations in his third edition show that he was ready to write for the times, and his practical purpose required that he should state his case in a fashion in which it would catch public attention. It was easier to discredit his opponents than to refute them by meeting them on their own ground or by showing that their position was untenable; and Adam Smith apparently sacrificed the part of a fair-minded critic, though he has certainly achieved the reputation of a great practical politician.

8. Secondly, the enthusiastic reception accorded to his work by his contemporaries was chiefly due to the extraordinary simplicity and clearness of his treatment, as well as to the excellence of the style. But this simplicity was secured by the definiteness of his new conception of the object of political economy. It had to do with the necessaries and conveniences of life, material commodities, definite concrete things. There was much clever compilation in the book, but it made no demand for additional inquiry as Massie had done, nor was much stress laid on that impalpable abstraction, the spirit of the nation; and the 'disagreeable discussion of metaphysical arguments' was avowedly abjured. It was all to be plain sailing for the man of ordinary intelligence; and within a few months of its publication the book had become a considerable power. In 1777 North had borrowed some suggestions which Adam Smith had incorporated from Moreau de Beaumont; Pitt's French policy followed the principles he had laid down,

and which he amplified in the edition of 1784; the great minister explicitly referred to the book in introducing his scheme for modifying the pressure of taxation in 1792, and was determined by it in his action on two later occasions. National prosperity and relative superiority were vague and difiicult notions, but when the whole discussion was made to turn on wealth, the treatment seemed to be more concrete and definite, and it took hold upon the public mind.

There were of course some economists who never really adapted their habits of thought in accordance with Adam Smith's principles. Playfair speaks of him with respect, but he continued to draw his beautiful diagrams of the Balance of Trade, as if he still thought it furnished a criterion of something. His Inquiry into the Permanent Causes of the Decline and Fall af Wealthy and Powerful Nations enumerates all sorts of influences, physical and moral; but fails to reach any very perspicuous conclusions. He admired The Wealth of Nations, but it seems to have left him unaffected. There is far more interest in the attitude of the hostile critics and the points which they singled out for attack.

(a) Governor Pownall, whose Letter was published some few months after The Wealth of Nations had been issued, subjected it to very acute criticism. He was prepared to admit that some of the colonial restrictions worked badly, but he defended the principle on which they rested, and which Adam Smith had ignored. Hs was prepared to relax restrictions that cause a roundabout trade, 'always however keeping in view this object and end namely, that so far as our colonies have to be considered as an institution, established sud directed to increase the naval force of our marine empire, and so far sa that force derives in any degree from the operations of their commercial powers, so in that monopoly which engrafts them upon our internal establishment, is indispensable and ought never to be departed from or relaxed.' In fact he held that the object of a 'political economy' was not merely any kind of wealth, but the maintenance of English power.

(b) Pownall also criticised Adam Smith's account of the production of wealth. In this he had apparently followed Locke. The fertility of this master mind is strangely shown in the fact that his writings contain the germ of the Physiocratic doctrine of taxation as well as the germ of Smith's doctrine of the production of wealth and the measure of value. 'Labour,' he had said, 'puts the difference of value on everything,' or as he corrects it, 'labour makes the far greater part of the value of things we enjoy,' but Adam Smith uses the principle in its most absolute form. In the first sentence of The Wealth of Nations, labour is spoken of as if it were the sole source of value, and therefore it is subsequently used as s measure of value. Against all this Pownall protested. 'Labour is not the measure of value but the mixture of the labour and the objects laboured upon which produces the composite value. The labour must remain unproductive, unless it hath some object whereon to exert itself.' There is no one commodity,' he adds, 'that will measure all others, but that all are to one another in their reciprocal value alternate measures, and that gold and silver is only the most common and most general, almost the universal measure.' 'Correlative value between commodities must depend upon, and derive from reciprocal higgling of bargain and sale, and are not measured by labour.' In accordance with this principle he urges that 'as there is no real measure of value so I think there is no fixed natural rate of value or real price distinct from the market price.'

(c) Similar criticisms were urged in a much less friendly spirit by Mr. Simon Gray in his own name, and under the somewhat thin disguise of George Purves. He is specially bitter on Adam Smith's distinction between productive and unproductive labour. He considered that Adam Smith's phraseology tended to foment class hatreds, as it seemed to represent all other classes as paupers who subsisted as mere drones and at the expense of the manual labourers. He argues in opposition that all labour is either directly or indirectly productive, and that the real question is who are more and who are less productive? But his chief point is that the cause of wealth lies not in mere labour, but in effective demand, a doctrine for which he argues with much acuteuess. There are necessary limitations which he does not sufficiently take into account, such as the law of diminishing return from land, and his optimistic conclusions are illusory; but none the less is his criticism exceedingly instructive, especially in the way he develops a doctrine of demand as determining supply. He gives far more scope to the idea of reciprocity than is found in most writers of his day.

9. Whatever may be thought of the worth of this contemporary criticism, it is of the first importance, since it helps us to understand the precise nature of Adam Smith's contribution to science. By isolating wealth as a subject for study he introduced an immense simplification. The investigation of economic phenomena was more definite, and just because he achieved this result his work rendered it possible to ask new questions, and so to make a real advance in every direction of social study. Not till we isolate wealth and examine how it is procured and how it may be used, can we really set about investigating how material goods may be made to subserve the highest ends of human life. National rivalries and national power are but mean things after all; but till the study of wealth was dissociated from these lower aims, it was hardly possible to investigate empirically how we could make the most of the resources of the world as a whole, and how material goods might be best applied for the service of man. It is owing to Adam Smith and the manner in which he severed economics from politics that we can raise and dismiss, even if we cannot solve, such problems to-day.

Similarly, we find the clearest testimony to his greatness in the new form which the old inquiries assumed. He severed economic science from politics; he dealt with it as concerned with physical objects and natural laws. To his English predecessors it had been a department of politics or morals; while many of his English successors recognized that in his hands it had become more analogous to physics and delighted to treat it by the methods of mechanical science. Whether consciously or unconsciously, he gave the turn to economic problems which has brought about the development of modern economic theory.

The progress that has been made in this direction amply justifies the line which Adam Smith took in isolating the study of material wealth; but however complete our analysis may be, it is well to remember that we have merely analysed a group of phenomena which we have first isolated as a matter of convenience. We cannot forecast at all unless we go outside economics and take a wider view of human life. For all questions of history in the past, for all questions of duty now, for all ideals of progress in the future we must not be content to take the phenomena of wealth as if they were isolated, but to take them in their relation to Man. For all these purposes we must seek to 'restore mind to its proper rank;' and even if there be no general formula which adequately describes the relations of moral phenomena to wealth, we may none the less hope to make good progress in all other sides of social study, if we use as our starting-point the vantage ground which Adam Smith has given us by isolating the conception of material wealth.

W. Cunningham

www.ingramcontent.com/pod-product-compliance
Lightning Source LLC
Chambersburg PA
CBHW071605170526
45166CB00004B/1809